PREPARATI

MUST-HAVE

- ☐ FLIGHT / BOAT / TRAIN TICKETS:

  ☐ ...   ☐ ...   ☐ ...   ☐ ...

- ☐ ACCOMMODATION:

  ☐ ...   ☐ ...   ☐ ...   ☐ ...

- ☐ PASSEPORT   ☐ VISA

- ☐ AT LEAST 2 CREDIT CARDS
  (TO KEEP IN 2 SEPARATE SPOTS IN CASE OF LOSS OR THEFT!)

- ☐ CASH   ☐ INSURANCE (PHONE : .. ..)

- ☐ CHARGERS   ☐ ADAPTORS

TOILETRY BAG

- ☐ SHOWER GEL / SOAP   ☐ ...

- ☐ SHAMPOO   ☐ ...

- ☐ ...   ☐ ...

- ☐ ...   ☐ ...

- ☐ ...   ☐ ...

- ☐ ...   ☐ ...

1

PREPARATION

EVERYTHING ELSE

☐ UNDERWEAR   ☐ SOCKS

☐ T-SHIRTS   ☐ SHORTS

☐ HAT   ☐ SWIMWEAR

☐ A LITTLE JACKET JUST IN CASE   ☐ FLIP FLOPS

☐ ...   ☐ ...

☐ ...   ☐ ...

☐ ...   ☐ ...

☐ ...   ☐ ...

☐ ...   ☐ ...

☐ ...   ☐ ...

☐ ...   ☐ ...

☐ ...   ☐ ...

☐ ...   ☐ ...

☐ ...   ☐ ...

☐ ...   ☐ ...

My Itinerary

Date	Place	Arrive	Depart	Things to see
.. / .. / ..	....	...	...	...
.. / .. / ..	....	...	...	...
.. / .. / ..	....	...	...	...
.. / .. / ..	....	...	...	...
.. / .. / ..	....	...	...	...
.. / .. / ..	....	...	...	...
.. / .. / ..	....	...	...	...
.. / .. / ..	....	...	...	...
.. / .. / ..	....	...	...	...
.. / .. / ..	....	...	...	...
.. / .. / ..	....	...	...	...
.. / .. / ..	....	...	...	...
.. / .. / ..	....	...	...	...
.. / .. / ..	....	...	...	...
.. / .. / ..	....	...	...	...
.. / .. / ..	....	...	...	...

BUDGET & EXPENSES

DATE	NAME	PRICE	DESCRIPTION / NOTES
.. / .. / ..	....	...	...
.. / .. / ..	....	...	...
.. / .. / ..	....	...	...
.. / .. / ..	....	...	...
.. / .. / ..	....	...	...
.. / .. / ..	....	...	...
.. / .. / ..	....	...	...
.. / .. / ..	....	...	...
.. / .. / ..	....	...	...
.. / .. / ..	....	...	...
.. / .. / ..	....	...	...
.. / .. / ..	....	...	...
.. / .. / ..	....	...	...
.. / .. / ..	....	...	...
.. / .. / ..	....	...	...
.. / .. / ..	....	...	...

DATE	NAME	PRICE	DESCRIPTION / NOTES
.. / .. / ..	....	...	...
.. / .. / ..	....	...	...
.. / .. / ..	....	...	...
.. / .. / ..	....	...	...
.. / .. / ..	....	...	...
.. / .. / ..	....	...	...
.. / .. / ..	....	...	...
.. / .. / ..	....	...	...
.. / .. / ..	....	...	...
.. / .. / ..	....	...	...
.. / .. / ..	....	...	...
.. / .. / ..	....	...	...
.. / .. / ..	....	...	...
.. / .. / ..	....	...	...
.. / .. / ..	....	...	...
.. / .. / ..	....	...	...
.. / .. / ..	....	...	...

Day 1.

PLANNING

THINGS TO DO

BEST MEMORIES

DO NOT FORGET

DAY 2

PLANNING

THINGS TO DO

BEST MEMORIES

DO NOT FORGET

DAY 3.

PLANNING

THINGS TO DO

BEST MEMORIES

DO NOT FORGET

DAY 4.

PLANNING

THINGS TO DO

BEST MEMORIES

DO NOT FORGET

Day 5.

PLANNING

THINGS TO DO

BEST MEMORIES

DO NOT FORGET

Day 6.

PLANNING

THINGS TO DO

BEST MEMORIES

DO NOT FORGET

DAY 7.

PLANNING

THINGS TO DO

BEST MEMORIES

DO NOT FORGET

DAY 8.

PLANNING

THINGS TO DO

BEST MEMORIES

DO NOT FORGET

DAY 9.

PLANNING

THINGS TO DO

BEST MEMORIES

DO NOT FORGET

DAY 10.

PLANNING

THINGS TO DO

BEST MEMORIES

DO NOT FORGET

DAY 11.

PLANNING

THINGS TO DO

BEST MEMORIES

DO NOT FORGET

DAY 12

PLANNING

THINGS TO DO

BEST MEMORIES

DO NOT FORGET

29

DAY 13.

PLANNING

THINGS TO DO

BEST MEMORIES

DO NOT FORGET

DAY 14.

PLANNING

THINGS TO DO

BEST MOMENTS

DO NOT FORGET

DAY 15.

PLANNING

THINGS TO DO

BEST MEMORIES

DO NOT FORGET

DAY 16.

PLANNING

THINGS TO DO

BEST MEMORIES

DO NOT FORGET

DAY 17.

PLANNING

THINGS TO DO

BEST MEMORIES

DO NOT FORGET

Day 18.

PLANNING

THINGS TO DO

BEST MEMORIES

DO NOT FORGET

Day 19.

PLANNING

THINGS TO DO

BEST MEMORIES

DO NOT FORGET

DAY 20.

PLANNING

THINGS TO DO

BEST MEMORIES

DO NOT FORGET

Day 21.

PLANNING

THINGS TO DO

BEST MEMORIES

DO NOT FORGET

Day 22

PLANNING

THINGS TO DO

BEST MEMORIES

DO NOT FORGET

Day 23.

PLANNING

THINGS TO DO

BEST MEMORIES

DO NOT FORGET

Day 24.

PLANNING

THINGS TO DO

BEST MEMORIES

DO NOT FORGET

DAY 25.

PLANNING

THINGS TO DO

BEST MEMORIES

DO NOT FORGET

DAY 26.

PLANNING

THINGS TO DO

BEST MEMORIES

DO NOT FORGET

DAY 27.

PLANNING

THINGS TO DO

BEST MEMORIES

DO NOT FORGET

Day 28.

PLANNING

THINGS TO DO

BEST MEMORIES

DO NOT FORGET

DAY 29.

PLANNING

THINGS TO DO

BEST MEMORIES

DO NOT FORGET

DAY 30.

PLANNING

THINGS TO DO

BEST MEMORIES

DO NOT FORGET

DAY 31.

PLANNING

THINGS TO DO

BEST MEMORIES

DO NOT FORGET

Day 32

Planning

Things to do

Best memories

Do not forget

DAY 33.

PLANNING

THINGS TO DO

BEST MEMORIES

DO NOT FORGET

Day 34.

PLANNING

THINGS TO DO

BEST MEMORIES

DO NOT FORGET

DAY 35.

PLANNING

THINGS TO DO

BEST MEMORIES

DO NOT FORGET

DAY 36.

PLANNING

THINGS TO DO

BEST MEMORIES

DO NOT FORGET

Day 37.

PLANNING

THINGS TO DO

BEST MEMORIES

DO NOT FORGET

Day 38.

PLANNING

THINGS TO DO

BEST MEMORIES

DO NOT FORGET

Day 39.

PLANNING

THINGS TO DO

BEST MEMORIES

DO NOT FORGET

DAY 40.

PLANNING

THINGS TO DO

BEST MEMORIES

DO NOT FORGET

Day 41.

PLANNING

THINGS TO DO

BEST MEMORIES

DO NOT FORGET

Day 42

Planning

Things to do

Best memories

Do not forget

Day 43.

PLANNING

THINGS TO DO

BEST MEMORIES

DO NOT FORGET

Day 44.

PLANNING

THINGS TO DO

BEST MEMORIES

DO NOT FORGET

DAY 45.

PLANNING

THINGS TO DO

BEST MEMORIES

DO NOT FORGET

DAY 46.

PLANNING

THINGS TO DO

BEST MEMORIES

DO NOT FORGET

DAY 47.

PLANNING

THINGS TO DO

BEST MEMORIES

DO NOT FORGET

DAY 48.

PLANNING

THINGS TO DO

BEST MEMORIES

DO NOT FORGET

101

DAY 49.

PLANNING

THINGS TO DO

BEST MEMORIES

DO NOT FORGET

DAY 50.

PLANNING

THINGS TO DO

BEST MEMORIES

DO NOT FORGET

DAY 51.

PLANNING

THINGS TO DO

BEST MEMORIES

DO NOT FORGET

DAY 52

PLANNING

THINGS TO DO

BEST MEMORIES

DO NOT FORGET

DAY 53.

PLANNING

THINGS TO DO

BEST MEMORIES

DO NOT FORGET

DAY 54.

PLANNING

THINGS TO DO

BEST MEMORIES

DO NOT FORGET

DAY 55.

PLANNING

THINGS TO DO

BEST MEMORIES

DO NOT FORGET

DAY 56.

PLANNING

THINGS TO DO

BEST MEMORIES

DO NOT FORGET

DAY 57.

PLANNING

THINGS TO DO

BEST MEMORIES

DO NOT FORGET

Day 58.

PLANNING

THINGS TO DO

BEST MEMORIES

DO NOT FORGET

DAY 59.

PLANNING

THINGS TO DO

BEST MEMORIES

DO NOT FORGET

DAY 60.

PLANNING

THINGS TO DO

BEST MEMORIES

DO NOT FORGET

Printed in Great Britain
by Amazon

24840955R00069